Other books in the Emotatude series by Karen Porter include:

The Compassion Emotatude
Fear Walking
Anne and Amy's Anger
How Gregory Deals with a Case of Grief
How to be Heebie Jeebie Free
The Secret of Warm Fuzzies
Controlling Kanipshun Fits
What to do When you get the Bejeebers Scared Out of You
Turtle one and Turtle Two

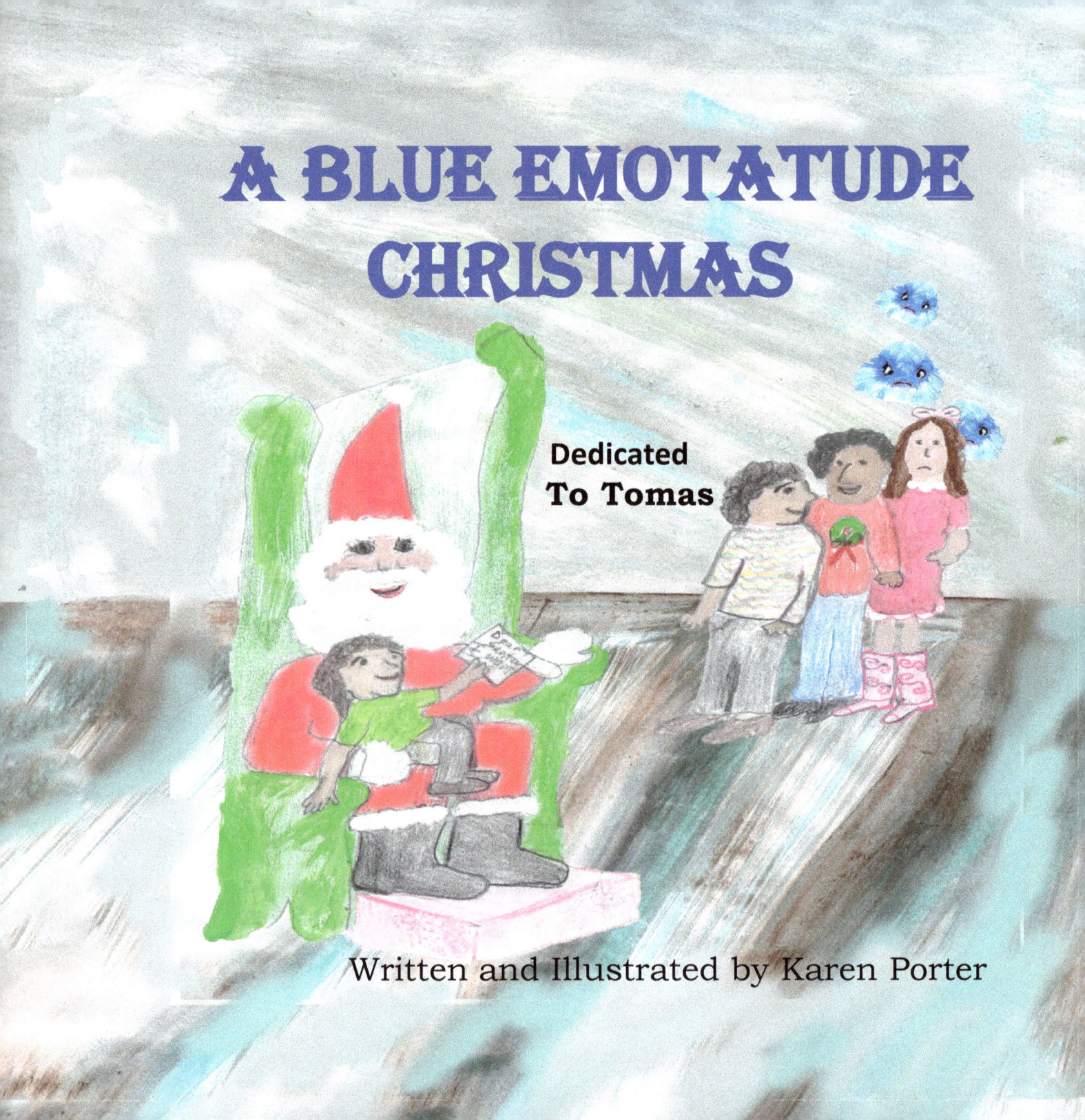

Emotatude Book

A Blue Emotatude Christmas

Coping with Depression During the Holidays
paperback version

KAREN PORTER

Copyright © 2021 Karen Porter., Everfield Press, Florida. All rights reserved. No part of this book shall be reproduced or transmitted in any form or means, electronic, mechanical, magnetic, photographic including photocopying, recording or by any information storage and retrieval system, without prior written permission of the author.

All rights reserved.

ISBN: 978-1-946785-37-4I

Wednesday, blues followed her into the cafeteria. Everyone was happily decorating Christmas tree cookies with sprinkles. She just did not care.

They followed her to the playground where all the kids licked the frosting off of their tree cookies. Eileen just felt blue.

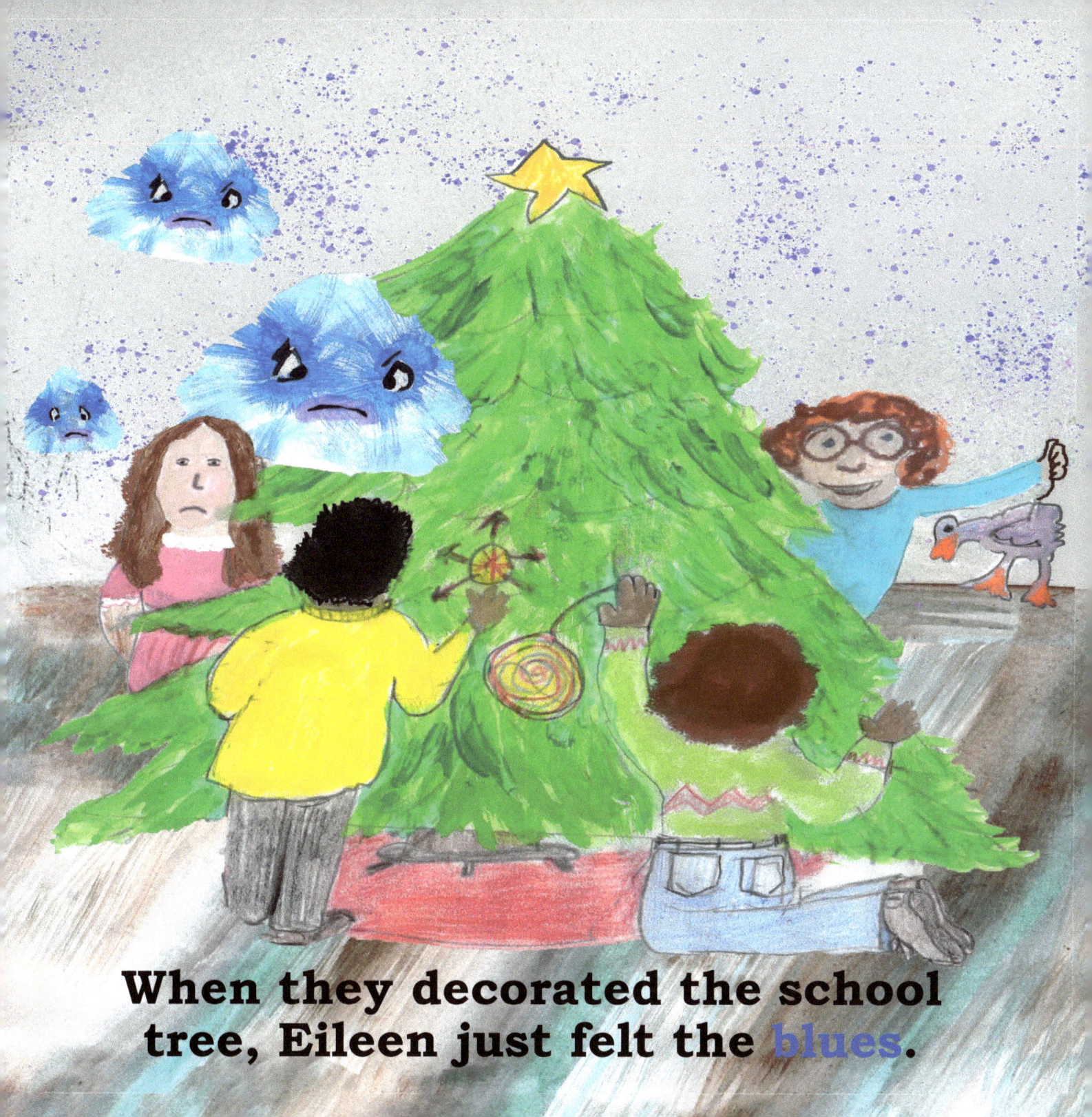

When they decorated the school tree, Eileen just felt the blues.

The blues watched Greg count the days left till Christmas.

When everyone shared their Christmas lists, Eileen didn't care. She couldn't think about what she wanted to give or get. She could only feel blue.

When all the other kids knew what they wanted for Christmas as they waited in line to sit on Santa's lap, Eileen just felt blue. She couldn't think about what to say to Santa.

When it was time to play Christmas songs in the band, everyone felt the joy of the season except for Eileen. She just... felt the blues.

The blues followed her to the store. Her mother was worried that she seemed too blue for a fun holiday like this.

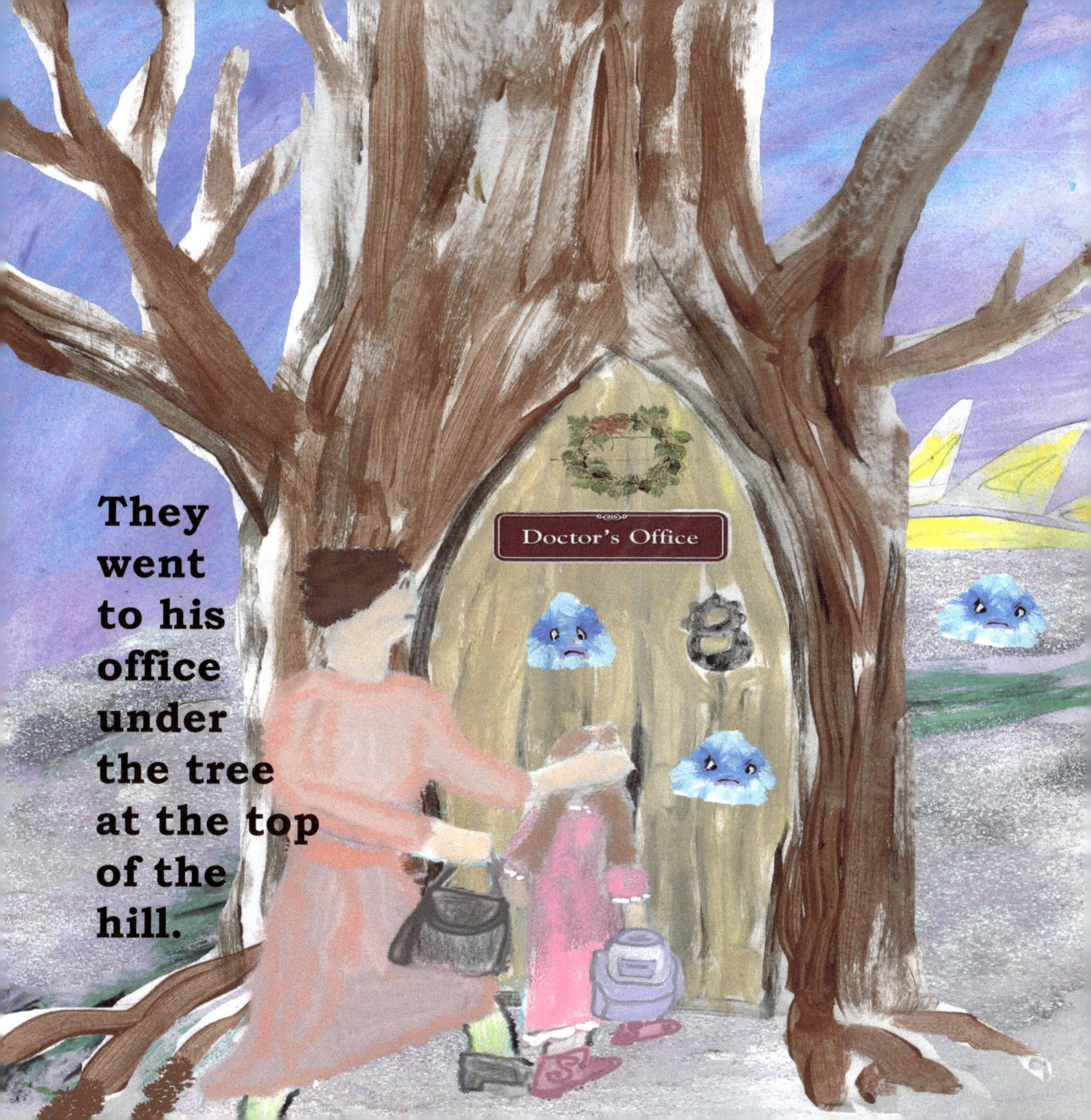
They went to his office under the tree at the top of the hill.

Dr. Kich looked at Eileen through his emotoculars. He said, "You have a big case of the blues! The blues must be following you everywhere you go! Come sit in my office and talk about it with me. I think I can help you cope with this."

She hugged her stuffed toy panda Xiao Ling every day. Her mom still worried about her when she went into her room and shut the door.

She played cards with her friend Jean. But her mother still worried about her when she went into her room and shut the door after the game was over.

She had a nice mug of hot chocolate every day. But her mother still worried about her when she went into her room and shut the door after the hot chocolate was finished.

Every time, after she tried to get rid of her blues, she went back into her room.

When the day for the appointment came Eileen's mother said, "Eileen, time to come out for your video conference with Dr. Kich."
"No, I am not ready.
I am doing something," Eileen replied.

Then her mother turned on the video conference with Dr. Kich and said, "I am sorry, Eileen won't come out of her room. She has been doing everything on the prescription you gave us, but she is spending a lot of time in her room. I worry about that. I will go knock on her door. Just a minute."

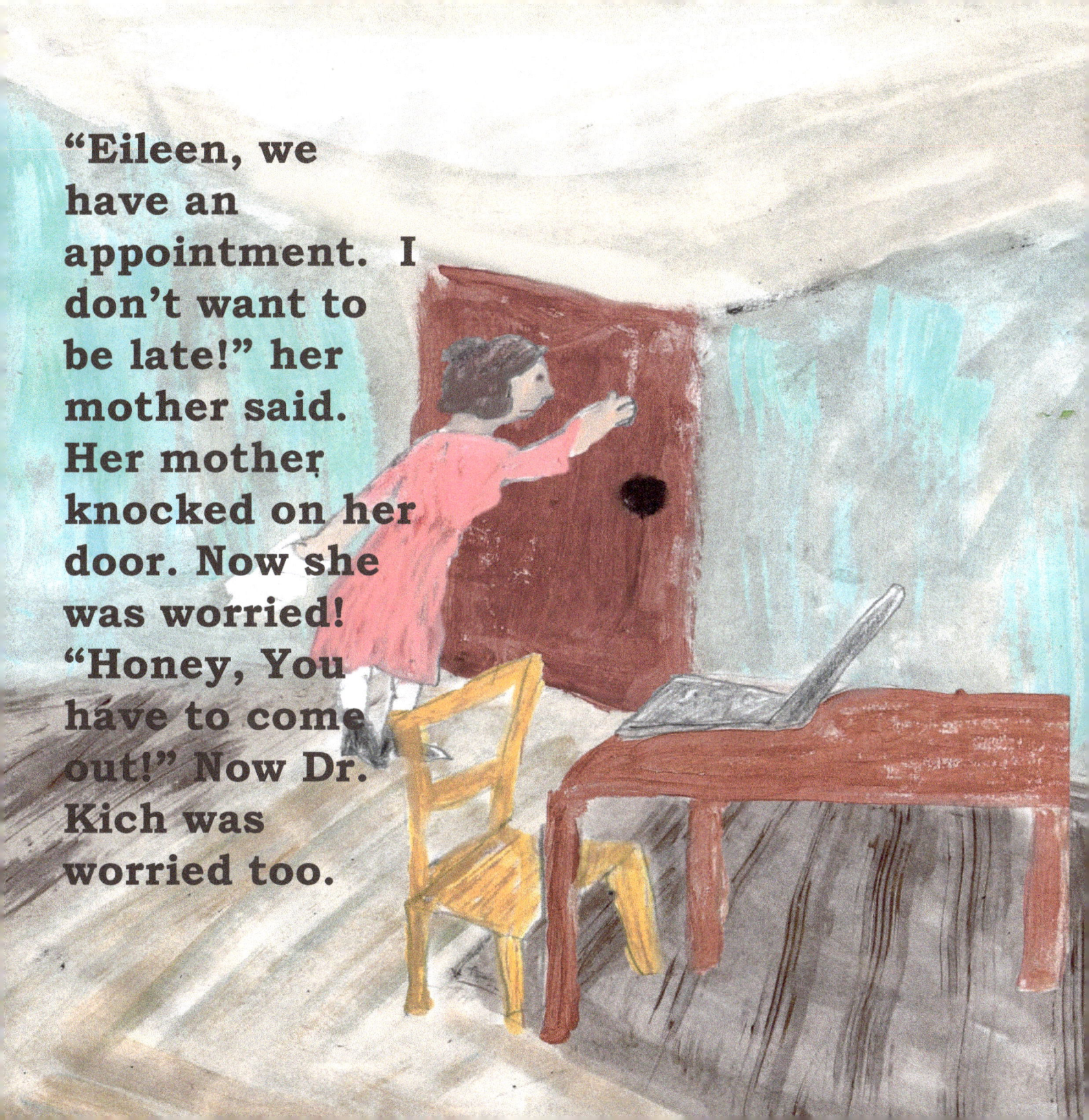

"Eileen, we have an appointment. I don't want to be late!" her mother said. Her mother knocked on her door. Now she was worried! "Honey, You have to come out!" Now Dr. Kich was worried too.

Suddenly the door opened. Eileen was smiling when she said, "I can work with my blues! They helped me decorate this Christmas tree."

They looked inside her room and saw ornaments with Eileen's blues shining brightly on the tree. Now she knew it was o.k. to show the world her blue feelings. They were blue and

Beautiful!

Note to parents

Sometimes we all just need a little time to process our feelings. This story was written to share that idea with others. If we allow our feelings to just be, as we explore them in healthy ways we can cope more efficiently. If we practice positive self care as we move through sadness, we can become more resilient people.

Vocabulary

Emotatude: A vibratory being that helps us feel our emotions.

Blues: A soul felt sadness.

Depression: The state of being in a sad mood for a prolonged period.

Emotocular: A device to enable an Emotologist to see Emotatudes.

Emotologist: A person who studies Emotatudes.

A Note from the Authors

Is Emotatudology Real? What is an Emotatude? According to the Emotatude children's book series, an Emotatude is a vibratory being that lives within us that brings forth an emotion we are having, and Emotatudology is the study of these vibratory beings. While the science of Emotatudology is purely fictional, many of the concepts proposed by the series' fictional character Dr. Kich are based on the real-world science of emotion and recent discoveries by scientists, energy healers, psychologists, and psychiatrists.

Promoting emotional agility is the aim of the Emotatude children's book series. Even though we can not literally touch, see, feel, hear, smell, and taste feelings, this concept helps children contemplate how feelings operate in their lives. Thus, we created the character Dr. Kich to personify the scientist in all of us who learns how to make sense of our emotional world through hypothesis testing, observation, theorizing, and drawing conclusions about our world. While Emotatudology as a revered established science is fictional, the concepts of how to deal with emotions are based on research, psychologists, biologists, and other scientists are currently researching. This is evident in the list of publications and organizations that are emerging in science.

If you feel blue this Christmas or any time consider making an expression tree like Eileen did. This way you can honor the feelings you have, and you can give them a place of honor in your home this season.

Questions For Readers

1. Have you ever been sad or blue?

2. Is it important to be happy all the time?

3. How does it feel to be blue when everyone else is happy?

4. Can you imagine anything that will cheer you up?

5. Do you think all feelings are important? Why or why not?

Karen White Porter is an Author and Illustrator of the 'Emotatude' series of children's books. She combines various mediums in her artwork such as pen and ink drawing, pencil, tempura, and other raised compounds to create an amalgam of colors that express feeling. Her work with children as a National and State certified teacher has given her insight into how young people look at emotion. It was through her teaching that she realized the importance of emotional intelligence among her students. Students from around the world gave her a fresh perspective of how emotional underpinnings affect the way all people learn.

One year Karen experienced a loss of a loved one around Christmas time. She realized it is important to go through the season and take care of yourself while authentically experiencing sadness during the holidays. This book is written for all people who may have difficulty dealing with sadness at Christmas.

www.ingramcontent.com/pod-product-compliance
Lightning Source LLC
Chambersburg PA
CBHW042357280426
43661CB00096B/1148